GET OFF MY BRAIN

A SURVIVAL GUIDE FOR LAZY STUDENTS

GET OFF MY BRAIN

A SURVIVAL GUIDE FOR LAZY STUDENTS

RANDALL McCUTCHEON

Foreword by Steve Allen
Illustrations by Pete Wagner

Free Spirit Publishing Co.
123 N. Third St., Suite 716
Minneapolis, MN 55401
(612) 338-2068

Library of Congress Cataloging in Publication Data

McCutcheon, Randall James, 1949-
  Get off my brain.

  Includes index.
  Summary: An illustrated guide to ways of improving study habits with suggestions for writing creative papers, making speeches, doing research, getting good grades, and time management.
  1. Study, Method of. 2. Underachievers. (1. Study, Method of) I. Wagner, Pete, ill. II. Title.
LB1049.M22   1985   371.3′028′12   84-82166
ISBN 0-915793-02-4

Printed in the United States of America

10   9   8   7   6   5   4

Cover design by Makela Design Works
Photographs by Steven Seitzer
Typesetting by Superior Graphics
Keyline by Mike Tuminelly

For my grandmother

Acknowledgements

Special thanks to these student contributors:

Preeta Bansal
Brian Chaffin
Val Gaddis
Amy Garwood
Cara Hansen
Tonja Holder
Katie Johnson
Tom Lyon
Sue Lyon
John Nielson
Craig Smith
Julie Uribe
John Vitek

TABLE OF CONTENTS

Foreword by Steve Allen

George Bernard Shaw's observation that it's a great pity youth is wasted on the young can certainly be applied to the process by which most of us become formally educated. Particularly at the college level, it seems to come at the most inopportune time, at least for many of us. Unless we have the good fortune to be addicted to reading, to thirst after knowledge for its own sake, or to be fascinated by a given subject, it is quite possible for us to complete four or more years at an institution of higher learning and yet remain remarkably ignorant.

Part of the reason is that just at the time we are supposed to become scholars we suffer the distraction of having to learn to become adults. We are, quite understandably, preoccupied with the opposite sex, the tiresome but quite necessary burden of soon earning a living, the uncomfortable sensation of for the first time having our prejudices called into question, not to mention the thousand-and-one diversions that American life forces upon us by means of television, radio, recordings, films, popular music, newspapers and magazines of dubious gravity, sports, election campaigns that often insult our intelligence, crimes, alarms, and assorted trivia.

Small wonder, then, that what is supposed to be true education is, for millions, a sort of comedy of errors.

To refer to only one example:

On February 15, 1983, the NBC television evening news carried a feature about the incredible ignorance of students at the University of Miami concerning matters of simple geography.

A survey of over 100 geography students showed that 42 percent didn't know where London was! Several thought Quebec was in Alaska. One student believed the Falkland Islands were off the coast of England. More than half couldn't find Chicago! Many weren't too sure what part of Europe France was in. Greenland was mistaken for Iceland. And half of those polled didn't know where Baja, California was. But the final insult was that 8 percent of the students couldn't place Miami on the map!

My wife and I were watching the dinner-hour newscast on which these distressing revelations were made. "Perhaps," she said, "since that school is in Miami, a lot of the students may be immigrants, who wouldn't know much about American geography and might have difficulty speaking English."

A moment later, as the camera showed some of the students in the class and others being interviewed, we realized that Jayne's charitable thought had no relevance to the situation: the faces shown were almost entirely Anglo. There were no foreign accents.

An isolated exception?

On the contrary, it is all too typical. Mountains of evidence—both in the form of statistical studies and personal testimonies—established that the American people are suffering from a new and perhaps unprecedented form of mental incapacitation for which I have coined the word "dumbth."

Well, if things are this bad—and only because of limitations of space is it impossible to establish here that they are far worse—then almost any constructively remedial weapon, including that of humor, ought to be resorted to, and fast.

A too-hasty reading of Mr. McCutcheon's argument might suggest that he is really giving tips on how to sneak by, pass tests with a minimum of study, or graduate with the least expenditure of energy. Not so, the author is obviously as interested as any other dedicated educator in producing students who have at least approached the limits of their potential. His playful, jocular approach will certainly interest students who would have reacted negatively to a more traditional approach. The few natural geniuses do not especially require McCutcheon's assistance. The few dolts are unlikely to profit by it.

But there are undoubtedly many others who will respond favorably to this tongue-in-cheek book, with its winning combination of wit and wisdom.

Steve Allen

11

INTRODUCTION

Education is not nearly as sudden as a massacre
but in the long run it is more deadly.

—Mark Twain

My grandfather used to say, "Yep...I went through school (a somewhat overly melodramatic pause) in the front door and out the back."

Since then I have heard too many students express the same sentiment. And they weren't joking.

In interviewing students about their school experiences, the following sentiments kept being repeated:

"School is such a waste of time."

Jon, 17

"Teachers and classes don't require students to think."

Kevin, 18

> "I get so bored in class that any motivation I had to begin with is soon lost. Then, I don't want to do anything in school."
>
> **David, 18**

> "I'm tired of being held back in school. In fact, I'm just tired."
>
> **Renee, 15**

Unfortunately for most of us, the resources that are available to ease the scholarly life of the lazy (i.e. unmotivated) student are sadly lacking. It is true that bookstore reference shelves are lined with study aids, but they invariably make the same false assumptions:

- **Students can study for several hours every night and still maintain their sanity.**

- **All students set specific long range goals and follow through with action.**

- **Research abilities are innate.**

- **All classes are equally interesting.**

- **Students are never incapacitated by personal crises, let alone adolescent mooncalfing or lollydolling.**

- **Students are willing to read hundreds of humorless pages written in tiresome prose to discover that being a "good" student is nearly impossible for a normal person.**

This study guide is nothing more than a simple attempt to change the course of academic history. And it is written for you . . . the normal, bright, lazy student.

But just exactly what is "lazy?" According to psychologist Dr. Thomas Greenspon, of Minneapolis, Minnesota, words like lazy may be descriptors for "those who choose not to do what we (teachers and parents), or society at large, think they should be doing."

The reasons for this unwillingness to conform (and perform) are as numerous as the people giving them. For example, some people are such perfectionists that everything must be just right in order for them to feel accepted.

I always think, 'I'm so intelligent therefore I should get A's no matter what the subject is.'
Missy, 17

People who do things in order to live up to the expectations of others, or who place unreasonably high goals for themselves, often simply stop trying. They become "lazy" so they no longer have to be perfect.

Students who breeze through the elementary school days may suffer from a lack of study skills when they reach more challenging classes. Simply showing up for class won't be enough anymore. If you find yourself in this situation, don't give in to the temptation to simply cop-out and use the excuse, "I'm just too lazy to do this work."

These are the Murphy's Law Lovers. If you fall into this category we recommend these (albeit corny,) words of inspiration:

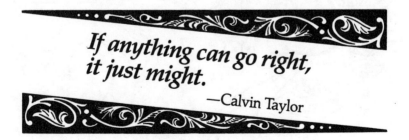

If anything can go right, it just might.
—Calvin Taylor

Finally, if you are lazy, remember you are not alone:

> "Lazy means always being depressed because you never get anything accomplished."
>
> *Janet, 17*

> "It is my favorite way of saying no!"
>
> *Mike, 15*

> **"Lazy:** (in-tel-ij-ent):(origin obscure, probably from Latin *G. Lazius Efortulus,* the only Roman who did not leave a twenty-volume collection of memories to plague future generations...best known for his famous query 'So what?') *Adj.* **1:** the condition or state of cleverness **2:** the extraordinary ability to meet life head down **3:** having sufficient willpower and stamina to avoid mundane drudgery while at the same time harvesting the fruits of mental inactivity *(See also 'coma')."*
>
> *Brian, 17*

'SO WHAT?'

With tongue-in-cheek and, most likely, head-on-pillow, these students have suggested the purpose of this book: To help you survive in school. And if the principles outlined in this guide are applied consistently and creatively, you will not only survive; you will thrive.

> # Creative minds have always been known to survive any kind of bad training.
> ## —Anna Freud

In the pages that follow, you will learn strategies that will make you more effective in the classroom—everything from how to amuse yourself in boring classes to how to improve your grade point average with less effort. And more importantly, how to actually learn something in school.

These strategies will work for you unless the symptoms of your laziness are related to more serious problems than those previously outlined. For example, if you have a *debilitating* fear of failure, suffer from a learning or physical disability that hasn't been appropriately dealt with, or have absolutely no support systems, the help you need demands more attention than this book can provide. Such obstacles need to be confronted with the help of trained professionals before you go any further with *Get Off My Brain*. If you suspect you need specialized assistance, RUN to the nearest counselor, psychologist, family physician, special education teacher or other trusted adult. Explain your concerns and get help in deciding what action should be taken.

For those of you just normally lazy, we begin now. Prepare yourself for the wonderful world of rest and relaxation awarded to students willing to learn to play the system.

The I-Get-So-Bored-Address

(With my apologies to one of our tallest presidents)

Nobody kept score and many cheers ago, our poor teachers brought forth the concept, conceived in mediocrity, that all students are created equal and therefore need only be equally creative.

Now we are engaged in a back-to-basics bedlam. We have made our bedlam, but it is the students who must lie in it. Therefore, it is altogether fitting and proper that we should stop lying.

But in a larger sense we can no longer demonstrate, we can no longer educate, we can no longer create in the classroom. The brave minds, dead and dying, who struggle there, may never create but they can add and subtract.

True, the world will little note nor long remember what we say here, but generations of students will be forced to memorize it verbatim and pass a true-false test. And so it is rather for us, the thinking, to abhor the dead minds and spreading behinds with our last full measure of revulsion: That we here highly resolve that there must be a new birth of free thinking, and that the creativity of the students, by the students, and for the students shall not perish from education.

If Abraham Lincoln was a young man today, forced to sit through semester after semester of high school or college classes, he probably would have remained a railsplitter.

Yes, friends, the uncivil war between teachers and students rages on. And emancipation is a futile flight of fancy, so you might as well begin preparing for battle.

We believe there are strategies you can employ to survive through even the deadliest of doldrums. To paraphrase Thoreau: *You must learn to march to the beat of a different doldrummer.* We suggest you experiment with these activities to fill those times when the teacher is unable, or you are unwilling, to fill your mind.

The Meaningless Question

This strategy involves getting the teacher sidetracked into discussing an irrelevant subject so that you can allow your mind to wander freely.

Two keys to success: A) Make sure that your question generates an answer that will not include testable material or you lose the game, and B) Carefully monitor the mood of the teacher so that your plan does not cause the teacher to become angry with you.

Here are some examples of "meaningless" questions:

"I've always wondered, how does school differ today from when you were a student?"*

"Since teachers are professionals—just like doctors and lawyers—why aren't they paid more money?"

---

*This type of question is best used before a serious discussion starts or near the end of the period when it is obvious that even the teacher is bored.

"In Shakespeare's play, Hamlet is confronted with the choice of 'to be or not to be.' When you were growing up, were you ever depressed enough to seriously consider suicide?"

(Please note, it is a safe bet that most teachers and professors have been seriously depressed—that seems to be a prerequisite for the job. And remember that this question will adapt to almost any poem, short story, or novel. Fortunately for you, most writers are always depressed, too.)

The beauty of this question is that it works for any subject. Simply delete "math" and and plug in the other possibilities.

Ramblin' Prose

This strategy, and the next one, require a willingness to speak, at length, in class. (Turn to pages 85-92 for suggestions on passing your "orals.") The trick is to pick an issue that is being discussed and see how long you can talk without being interrupted by another student or the teacher. Keep track of your progress, recording your times and an evaluation of your fluency in a special notebook.

Again, we must warn you that this works best when the mood is right. It is interesting to note, however, how many teachers appear grateful not to have to teach. Proceed with caution.

The Fake Argument

This strategy requires being in cahoots with a fellow classmate. All you do is wait for a controversial issue to be discussed in class. Immediately one of you should make a strong statement defending a position (e.g. on the subject of capital punishment.)

"Anyone who commits an intentional felony should be shot!"

Then the other, just as quickly, contradicts the thesis of the first position:

"Anyone who would make a ridiculous statement like that should be shot!"

The argument continues from there until someone interrupts you, at which time you record in your notebook the results of your latest effort.

As before, the same precautions apply. In addition, we warn you not to let the logic of your arguments, or the intense passion with which you present them, offend the teacher's sensibilities.

Leave Skipping to Lou

Clearly, you cannot experiment with the aforementioned activities unless you attend class. You cannot learn either. So if amusing yourself with these strategies is not enough incentive to get you to class, then consider the following independent reasons:

◆ The teacher's ego can be your downfall. Many teachers have gone on to achieve M.A. and Ph.D. degrees. That takes sacrifice. When you skip class, some teachers take that to mean you are questioning the importance of their work. It is an insult to them. It is rejection. In short, they won't like you. Often they will find a way to punish you. Lower grades, for example.

> "Coming to class is essential. As soon as the teacher becomes aware of how much you care, you will be subject to the same treatment the other students have been receiving all along."
> **Josh, 15**

> "Some students are careful not to answer *too many* questions in class so others won't think them 'teacher's pet' or 'goody goody.' But I have to admit that participating a lot in class helps to alleviate boredom. Besides, students don't give out the grades."
> **Missy, 18**

◆ Many teachers test out of their notes. We have discovered a correlation between a teacher's subject intelligence level and the need to study lecture notes. In other words, the more the teacher knows, the less likely there is a need to rely on the textbook to create questions for the test. With a little research and an educated guess, you can determine where to allocate your limited study time. Sometimes you may not need to read the textbook at all. (For more tips on test taking, see pages 93-104.)

◆ You will understand the notes better if *you* take them. The classic rationalization, "Oh, I don't need to go to class today, I'll just borrow Johnny's notes," demonstrates how naive you are about the process of understanding both complex explanations and Johnny.

◆ Your attendance and careful note-taking decrease the need for outside study. Normally, borrowed notes or a short recapitulation in study hall or back at the dorm do not give a clear assessment of what material was most important to learn. The teacher, through non-verbal clues and various asides (e.g. "That Freudian application I just explained for the last 20 minutes is just for your own edification and will not be on the test!"), suggests areas on which to focus your study efforts. Do your friends write down these clues and asides? Don't make us laugh.

Sit In The Front Row

> Nine-tenths of the people were created so you would want to be with the other tenth.
>
> **—Horace Walpole**

There is no reason to cheat off the student sitting next to you when you can tap his or her talents through the legitimate use of logistics. In other words, put up a good front by sitting up front.

• You will often meet brighter, even more gifted and ambitious students than yourself by sitting in the front row. It is true that the academically gifted are likely to plop down anywhere; but a higher percentage, row-wise, will be near the teacher. If you're in college, you'll note graduate students inevitably gravitate in that direction. Make friends with these people, play up to them, pat their heads, give them your full attention.

A "BELL CURVE" SEATING CHART.

- What does this mean for you? These front row students are more likely to take good notes that you can borrow, if you absolutely must miss class (reread pages 23 & 24). If you don't understand some of the lecture material and the teacher is usually busy after class, these students are the next best thing. Plus, these students will be able to provide superior insight when trying to second-guess potential test questions.

- You are less likely to fall asleep. Snoring is visible, noisy, and later, embarrassing. In the large lecture halls of colleges, the back rows are reserved for football players, their sorority kittens, the fraternity party cretins, and others of their ilk who bring with them only crowds of gloom.

- By sitting up front, you give the teacher a chance to get to know you. If he is at all approachable, you have, as they say headed off the other students at the pass (and passing, after all, is the name of the game). Clearly, if the teacher is prone to fits of gabbiness—then it is a simple matter to introduce yourself, and at the same time, remove yourself from the stigma of being just another number.

- It is a good idea to choose your position in the front row next to a student that you are certain the teacher likes. Remember the childhood advice not to sit too close to the fire (meaning naughty students) or you would get burned? Well, a corollary is true—sit by likeable, bright students and you will get en-light-ened.

• When you sit in the front row your confidence level will increase. Besides the obvious merits of no guilt trip for skipping out or falling asleep, it is likely you will feel more positive when studying for exams if you have attended and listened. A positive attitude can be critical in passing the threshold of trying, and thus, in passing the class.

Random Thoughts

At some point(s) in your career as a student, emotional trauma will interfere with your desire to attend class, perhaps even with your desire to move. You will begin to question the meaning of life and the need to be responsible. You will not sleep much, if at all. For many students this is when the G.P.A. (grade poop average) hits the fan.

Ah, sweet romantics, lazy learners, fellow passengers on that ship of foolish behavior—your ship, your future, is sinking.

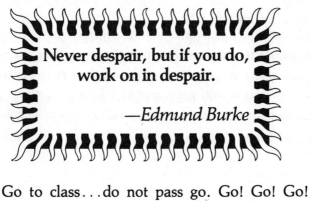

Never despair, but if you do, work on in despair.

—*Edmund Burke*

Go to class...do not pass go. Go! Go! Go! If you don't, you may not end up in jail; but you won't end up owning your own monopoly either.

Finally, in selecting classes, whenever possible, choose by teacher not by course. Try to match your personality and learning style with the personality and teaching style of each prospective teacher.

> **"Socrates once advised to 'know thyself'**
> **which explains why he was the teacher."**
> *Amy, 17*

Learning Styles

For example, it makes little sense to choose a teacher who gives only essay questions if your preference is for the objective test. Nor does it make sense to register for a boring lecturer if the same class is taught by "Mr. Movie" and his Encyclopaedia Britannica film library.

If you aren't familiar with the concept of learning styles, or aren't sure in which ways you learn best, spend time doing a bit of research and self-assessment. A few hours of pre-semester soul searching, interviews with former students, and the completion of personality "Prof . . . iles" (see pages 41—48) can save weeks of torture, tongue-biting, and tedium.

In assessing your learning style, we suggest you look at the work of Anthony F. Gregorc, Ph.D. and Kathleen A. Butler, Ph.D. Both have spent years studying the ways people learn, communicate, and relate to others. We believe the concept is well-researched and worth exploring. But don't take our word for it. Here's what students who have studied learning styles have to say about it:

"Studying learning styles helped me understand why some teachers, (who don't teach to my style,) frustrate me."

Nancy, 17

"Knowing about learning styles helps me to transcend difficult situations and difficult people."

Mark, 16

"Now I finally have an excuse for starting my homework at 10:00 on a Sunday night."

Sandy, 17

"It helped me realize how well-rounded I really am."

Jade, 15

Gregorc defines learning style as "outer behaviors which serve as indicators of a person's mediation abilities and capacities. It also provides clues as to how a person's mind operates." In other words, how you think and learn.

Gregorc and Butler discuss four major learning style types. They point out that all of us have some of the features of each style, yet most people exhibit dominant characteristics from one of these categories. The pages that follow provide an abbreviated version of Dr. Butler's "Styles Summary Chart."

If you are intrigued and want the complete chart, or more information on learning styles in general, write: Dr. Kathleen Butler in C/O Gabriel Systems, Inc., Box 357, Maynard, MA 01754.

CONCRETE SEQUENTIAL

Natural abilities include:

Working step-by-step
Planning, organizing
Following directions
Creating practical products
Getting the facts

CS's learn best when they:

Have an orderly environment
Face predictable situations
Can trust others to follow through
Can apply ideas in a practical way
Are given approval for specific work

CS's may have trouble:

Choosing from many options
Acting without specific rules
Understanding feelings
Answering "what-if" questions
Dealing with opposing views

To expand their style, CS's need to:

Express their own feelings
Not react to first impressions
Get explanations of others' views
Work with an organized divergent thinker
Set reasonable limits on expectations

This abbreviated version of the *Learning Styles Summary Chart* is reprinted by permission, Gabriel Systems, Inc. © Copyright, 1984, Kathleen A. Butler, Ph. D.

Abstract Sequential

Natural abilities include:

- ☐ Debating points of view
- ☐ Gathering information, analyzing ideas
- ☐ Being a patient learner
- ☐ Judging value or importance
- ☐ Finding answers

AS's learn best when they:

- ☐ Have access to references and experts
- ☐ Follow traditional procedures
- ☐ Can work alone
- ☐ Are respected for intellectual ability
- ☐ Rely on lecture notes and do library research

AS's may have trouble:

- ☐ Working in groups effectively
- ☐ Writing creatively
- ☐ Being criticized
- ☐ Facing the unpredictable
- ☐ Convincing others diplomatically

To expand their style, AS's need to:

- ☐ See the humorous side of life
- ☐ Accept imperfection
- ☐ Place grades in perspective
- ☐ Explore personal feelings
- ☐ Consider alternatives, choices

Abstract Random

Natural abilities include:

✘ Having the ability to reflect
✘ Being flexible
✘ Being sensitive
✘ Having an imagination and using it to create
✘ A preference for being part of a group

AR's learn best when they:

✘ Can work & share with others
✘ Have assignments requiring interpretation
✘ Balance work with play
✘ Have a noncompetitive atmosphere
✘ Can communicate with others

AR's may have trouble:

✘ Giving exact answers
✘ Memorizing
✘ Working within time limits
✘ Organizing parts
✘ Focusing on one thing at a time

To expand their style, AR's need to:

✘ React less emotionally to time limits
✘ Look before they leap
✘ Attend to important details
✘ Stick with a decision & follow through
✘ Include objective data in making decisions

This abbreviated version of the *Learning Styles Summary Chart* is reprinted by permission, Gabriel Systems, Inc. © Copyright, 1984, Kathleen A. Butler, Ph. D.

Concrete Random

Natural abilities include:

* Experimenting to find answers
* Creating change
* Independence
* Curiosity
* Creating unusual approaches

CR's learn best when they:

* Are self-directed
* Use trial-and-error approaches
* Produce real, yet imaginative, products
* Are competitive
* Use open-ended activities

CR's may have trouble:

* Pacing, meeting time limitations
* Choosing one answer
* Keeping detailed notes
* Following a lecture with no chance for interaction
* Having few options or choices

To expand their style, CR's need to:

* Learn to prioritize
* Bring projects to fruition
* Delegate responsibility
* Accept others' ideas as they are
* Not make promises they can't keep

This abbreviated version of the *Learning Styles Summary Chart* is reprinted by permission, Gabriel Systems, Inc. © Copyright, 1984, Kathleen A. Butler, Ph. D.

Keep in mind that there are no right or wrong, good or bad learning styles. There are simply different ways of looking at and doing things. The most successful students learn to arrange schedules and assert themselves so they can learn in their most natural and effective style as often as possible. But when you can't have it your way, challenge yourself to stretch your limits and incorporate other style characteristics as well, (known as "style flex-ability" by Dr. Gregorc).

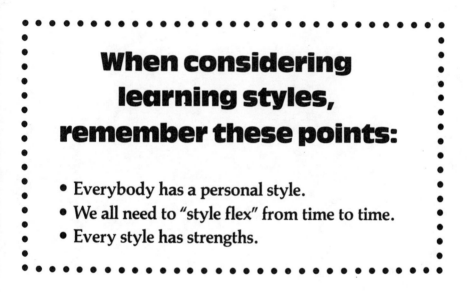

When considering learning styles, remember these points:

- Everybody has a personal style.
- We all need to "style flex" from time to time.
- Every style has strengths.

Nobody "Brown-Nosed" The Trouble I've Seen

The most important thing in acting is honesty.
Once you've learned to fake that, you're in.

—Sam Goldwyn

So far, we've tried to persuade you, among other things, to attend class, be sensitive to your learning style strengths, and to sit in the front row. Now we're ready to begin to refine our tactics.

Always smile and at least pretend to be interested. One student we interviewed even received a public thank you as a result of his efforts in this direction: "There is one student in this class that makes teaching a reward for me. Each session he is all smiles, and it lifts my spirits." The teacher went on to thank the student by name.

Most teachers will never get around to publicly thanking you; but they do notice your behavior, and they do remember.

? Ask only questions the teacher can answer. (There are exceptions but play the odds.)

**THE TIME TO POSE YOUR INQUIRY IS WHEN YOU OBSERVE THE INSTRUCTOR BECOMING MORE ANIMATED, EYES BURNING WITH CRANIAL CRAVING, FISTS FLAILING THE PODIUM, THREE DOLLAR WORDS HURTLING TOWARD THE IONOSPHERE.
OR MAYBE JUST A LITTLE BIT EXCITED.**

You can tell when a teacher knows what he or she is talking about. Ask your question then. Request that she amplify, explain more. Let her know you suffer from the same hunger.

Ask for information after class. Find out your teacher's classroom or office hours and discreetly pass by daily until you observe that he or she doesn't appear to be busy. Now is the time to strike because the teacher is probably looking for something to do anyway. Pick your favorite discussion topic and ask where you can find more information. Be specific. Ask for appropriate journal articles, studies, etc. You don't actually have to read the material; but, who knows, you might learn something.

Keep in mind that some teachers have little or no sense of humor. Some even maintain that you can have a good time memorizing the Periodic Table of the Elements, reading the Preamble to the Constitution, or figuring out what "x" is. Don't try to amuse these people. Their lives have gone the way of vaudeville.

Always be supportive of other students in the class. Overly competitive, grade mongering students who put others down in an attempt to elevate their own position are repugnant to most teachers. Compliment your classmates openly and often, but only when it is deserved. The teacher will be impressed by your generosity. One fringe benefit of a systematic approach to niceness is that sometimes it is contagious.

Random Thoughts

For those cynics among you, who are not easily convinced, let us remind you of a lesson to be learned by watching reruns of "Leave It To Beaver."

In one particular episode, Whitey and Beaver are raking Miss Lander's (their teacher's) yard. Whitey asks "The Beav" if he isn't worried about some of the guys thinking that they are trying to "butter-up" Miss Landers. Beaver replies, "My father says it doesn't matter what other people think of you, only what you think of yourself."

And we all know, cliché or no cliché, Ward Cleaver was never wrong.

Personality "Prof"...iles

Most teachers and professors, sooner or later, will reveal what their lousy childhoods were like and all that other David Copperfield kind of crap (even if they haven't read J.D. Salinger). These revelations provide a golden opportunity for you to enter the final transition from "gummer" to "gumshoe." To paraphrase Dragnet's Sgt. Joe Friday, "It's your job. You're a student."

You should take Sgt. Friday's advice. (Remember what happened to the lugheads and lamebrains who didn't?) Make your report card a decent place for grades to settle and raise your young average. And you may actually find yourself learning more than ever before in school.

How? Like any good detective, first, you should investigate, get the facts. Unfortunately, there will be times when you won't know what the facts mean. Teachers seem to delight in making references to obscure authors, unfamiliar events, and social causes that were unimportant even to their generation.

You must not allow yourself to become discouraged. Instead, you must dig to discover the background information necessary to apply these references in your course work and mediate your learning style with their teaching style. (After all, you can't expect them to change.)

To aid you in your beginning investigations here is a sample "prof"...ile that a student might have compiled from a few weeks of careful listening in my class.

Personality "Prof"...ile

(The inside Dope On That Dope McCutcheon)

TEACHING STYLE

Evidence

Except for the "Most Things In Life Should Be Organized Like A Bowling Team" speech, the lectures have been content-centered.
Prefers debating ideas to general class discussion.
Reinforces students who demonstrate use of logic and reasoning.

Conclusions

Style could best be categorized as Abstract Sequential.
Essays should be analytical as well as creative.
Need original research to support theories—won't buy "seat of the pants" assertions.
Must be willing to argue issues orally.
Most receptive to making judgements based on a synthesis of available information.

LITERATURE

Evidence (authors mentioned or quoted)

Poets: T.S. Eliot, Emily Dickinson, e e cummings, Lawrence Ferlinghetti, Dylan Thomas
Playwrights: Harold Pinter, John Guare, Jules Feiffer
Novelists: Max Shulman, J.D. Salinger, F. Scott Fitzgerald

Conclusions

This guy either reads all the time or is one of those name droppers.
Tendencies toward black comedy, abstraction, and romanticism dictate his reading habits.
Using literary references in papers for his classes would be an effective strategy.

MUSIC

Evidence

Singers/Songwriters: Bob Dylan, Beatles, Simon &
Garfunkel, Randy Newman.

Conclusions

Symptoms of chronic "flower childness."
Lyrics are important to him so quoting songs would
be effective in completing assignments.
Sixties folk rock would seem to be safest bet for consistent appeal.

POLITICS

Evidence

Statements in class are apolitical but have slight liberal leaning. However,
preferences in literature and music reveal stronger liberal commitment.
His agreeing with the observation that democracy will never work
because you can't have "wisdom through collective ignorance" is telling.

Conclusions

Never risk a hard-line conservative position on any issue.

RELIGION

Evidence

No statement - never discusses the topic.

Conclusions

He might be a typical Midwestern pseudo-intellectual who fancies himself an agnostic, or a pantheist. (The slip about golfing on Sunday mornings was curious.)
Staying away from religious doctrinaire would be the safest strategy.

SENSE OF HUMOR

Evidence

Laughs easily, sometimes when nothing funny is said or happening.
Doesn't like crude humor. He was visibly upset at a student who told an off-color story.
He never tells standard or formula jokes but seems to relish spontaneous puns or other types of creative word play.

Conclusions

The more humor in assignments the better. (Restrictions— be original, be clean.)
Most impressed by the "disassociated" ideas technique so use whenever possible.
Use of off-the-wall and black comedy are appropriate.

The secret to a successful "Prof"...ile investigation is in the application of the gathered material in fulfilling homework and test obligations. The following examples illustrate how the information from a "Prof"...ile can be used in answering essay questions.

If you were taking a psychology class, you might be given the following assignment: Write a short theme on the topic "Couples break-up as communication breaks down."

Before you commit a single word to paper, you study the "Prof"...ile revelations and choose T.S. Eliot's "Love Song of J. Alfred Prufrock" for an introductory passage.

"Would it have been worthwhile
> *If one, settling a pillow or throwing off a shawl*
> *And turning toward the window, should say:*
> *'That is not it at all,*
> *That is not what I meant at all.'"*

Then, as you explain the communication gap that separates some couples, sprinkle in lines from Paul Simon's song, "The Dangling Conversation." Your conclusion returns to your original choice of T.S. Eliot, and you end with this final quoted passage.

"till human voices wake us, and we drown."

If you were taking a theology course, you might be given the following essay question on your final exam.

Because you knew all along that this was a religion course, you have prepared by memorizing three generic approaches to any possible question on the subject. You have studied the "Prof" . . .ile, and you have chosen the Beatles' "Eleanor Rigby," Bob Dylan's, "With God on Our Side," and "Sometime During Eternity," a poem by Lawrence Ferlinghetti. Again, you take the lines from one of these works and create a structural vehicle that specifically addresses the question. (For imaginative ways to create these vehicles see pages 71-79.)

Random Thoughts

Finding links between your particular "Prof". . .ile and your actual course is not as difficult as it may seem at first. You must do some brainstorming and a little research, but big payoffs on grades are assured. Here are a few more examples to demonstrate that the ideas exist. You just have to find them.

Business—the Beatles' "Taxman"

Sociology—Paul Simon's "At the Zoo"

Art—Ferlinghetti's "One of the paintings that would not die"

Political Science—Randy Newman's
"Political Science"

Math—Godel, Escher, Bach, *An Eternal Golden Braid* by Douglas R. Hofstadter

Science—Alvin Toffler's *Future Shock*
Carl Sagan's *Cosmos*

Physical Education—John Updike's "ex-Basketball Player" or e e cummings' "nobody loses all the time"

Of course, the underlying assumption of this section is that all of your professors will have a personality. Let us pray.

All Work and No Wordplay

Many years ago, a distressed teacher described her recurring nightmare to fellow teachers. And although the details had long since faded from memory, the central image remained.

In this nightmare, the teacher found herself surrounded by hundreds of hands—no children—just their hands. Each hand grabbed at her, tugging at her, slowly dragging her down, until she collapsed.

Certainly, one of the rewards for teachers is the satisfaction of knowing that they have helped another human being to learn. (Leading a student to what David Brinkley observed in another context—"the dark at the end of the tunnel.") However, like our distressed teacher, *most* teachers believe they give much more than they receive.

This constant giving has been referred to as the process of emptying one's bucket. The teacher dips into the bucket and quenches the students' thirst for knowledge. This raises the obvious question: Who refills the teacher's bucket?

The answer is simple. You should! And you should refill that bucket with cheap thrills. In creative and constructive ways, you should try to bring some entertainment into teachers' otherwise routine, academic lives.

Consider the following ideas as just a few of the possible bucket fillers. Then use your imagination and profit from the teacher's overflowing gratitude.

Variations On A Theme

Try to put yourself in the professor's shoes, or if you will, at his desk. In front of you is a pile of thirty essays, all on the same subject. Remember these essays are not written by Alexander Pope or Walt Whitman. These essays are best described as the "literary poop" of your dim-witted classmates. That's right, after this ordeal, the ol' bucket is going to be bone dry.

The creative student will assess the open-mindedness of the instructor and change the assignment enough to make his or her paper different from the others. With luck, it may even be entertaining.

Here is an example based on an assignment that has now become a cliché in academic circles. The essay was to be titled, "What I Did Last Summer."

You vary the assignment and write, "What I Did Next Summer." In essence, you are projecting yourself into the future but are using past tense in the treatment. The focal point of your work might be an analysis of last summer's mistakes as a basis for future decision making.

This unusual approach, still related to the basic expectations of the assignment, will make your paper memorable.

Parodies

A clever, but often time consuming effort is to write both what is required by the assignment and a parody of your attempt. Admittedly, this takes some thought; but the teacher will usually recognize and reward that extra effort.

Suppose that you were instructed to write a paper on the style of Ernest Hemingway, as reflected in the novel, *A Farewell To Arms*. You might also turn in the following parody of Hemingway's style.

Title: A Farewell To Compounds
Note: This "farewell" was written while riding on a deserted stretch of
    beach. (My horse helped, too.)

Many things haven't happened and things don't happen all the time
and still it feels good to go on and never be unfaithful, that is almost
never and hardly ever killing anything you want and killing any damn
thing else clean and cleaning compound fractures of soldiers lonely in
military compounds and after all, it was a hell of a war and so you write
detached and unattached and unelated and usually unrelated...

And she was gone into darkness and more hardboiled nights and more
romantic bastards searching and eating, drinking, and being merry
welshing bottles full of hooch and autos full of girls very pretty and very
modest and very wifely and Los Angeles was a very young city and we
were very young and very, very and one and one was one and life was
simple then and math was simple then and one was still one and compound love interest made two and in two nights death parted us for
better and for worse and she returned far worse to dust and I returned to
chemical compounds far better...

And you can stop your story the way you stop a life and you do not
do it and afterwards you are not sorry and all of which and none of
which has anything to do with glory and honor and courage and booting
empty beer cans in Ketchum, Idaho and the judgment comes and the
compound sentence is served and sixty-two years turns into a life and
then one day you run out of... "ands."

It should be pointed out that this parody was written without
the benefit of having ever read a page of Mr. Hemingway's. The
strategy, instead, was to read two short passages of literary criti-
cism of his style and then exaggerate the described characteristics.

Letters To The Editor

This seldom used avenue of expression has the potential to impress all of your teachers at once. The trick to writing a successful letter to a campus "rag" or local newspaper is to attack, in a satirical vein, some issue that you know will meet the approval of your "average" academician. You can always say nay to the niggardly nature of those nattering nabobs of negativism who refuse to pay your poor professors even a poverty level pittance. A letter guaranteed to make you popular. Or you could try variations of the following letter in which this "universal appeal" strategy has been used.

 Time For Advice

Dear Editor:

Early Monday evening as I was leaving Love Library, I was accosted by what was clearly a tubbed, grubbed and freshly scrubbed freshman. Like most freshmen, he maintained the alert countenance of a recently gaffed salmon.

"Where are the football stadium?" he twanged. (Wrong verb conjugation. . .hmmmm. . .I wondered if his last name might be "Devaney.")

"It are that-a-way," I countered. He then countered up to 10 to prove that he could do it, and the conversation continued.

"Son," I began, "there is more to life than football."

He mulled over that morsel momentarily. "Yep! There's keggers, too."

Being the glutton for punishment that I am, I pressed on. "But what about the Performing Arts Series at Kimball, the plays at Howell, the foreign films?"

Back to the old mullstream-of-consciousness. "Yep! There's keggers, too."

Alas, I thought, it is time for more desperate measures. Fatherly advice.

"Son," I began again, "college is a lot like a football game. You chase a sheepskin instead of a pigskin, you gain knowledge instead of yardage, and you never violate the rules or sorority girls. Or was it the other way around?"

It was evident that my strained analogy was also straining him. So finally, to make a short story long and sensing the inevitability of his freshmen fate, I resorted to realism.

"Son," I began again, again, "you need never despair that your education will interfere with football. The regents, state legislators, and other warm-hearted buffoons will never allow the University of Nebraska to become the "Harvard of the Plains." Their pride in the Cornhuskers is matched only by their pride in ignorance. (There is nothing quite as profoundly moving as the wheezing sigh of a freshman silhouetted against a magnificent Nebraska sunset.)

"In fact, you can write Mom tonight and tell her that now you have struggled through your first classes, you are one day closer to the opening kick-off of the "Big Red Schoolhouse of the Astroturf."

Random Thoughts

Occasionally, you will need to make an excuse for an absence, a late paper, a low test grade. Be entertaining. Make even your excuses pleasantly memorable.

Val and Norman, two junior high school students, help us illustrate how this can be accomplished.

During class one day, Val wadded into a small ball the paper on which Norman had faithfully completed his math homework. Norman, although a tad irate, scribbled on the crumpled remains, "Val did this to my paper."

Val, observing this telltale message, and knowing the die was cast, created the perfect solution. Immediately, he wadded his own paper and penciled on his crumpled remains, "Norman did this to my paper."

There is a lesson here which should not escape you as you move on to higher education. In the world of excuses, it is best to be imaginative. In grade school it was acceptable to offer the flimsy, "My sister drew pictures all over my paper," or the improbable, "My dog ripped it apart." Now that you are older and must face teachers who are callous and inflexible, when forced to invent a rhyme or reason, try to use the old beanie:

"I'm sorry about the late paper, prof., but my dog, rather artistically I might add, ripped my sister apart."

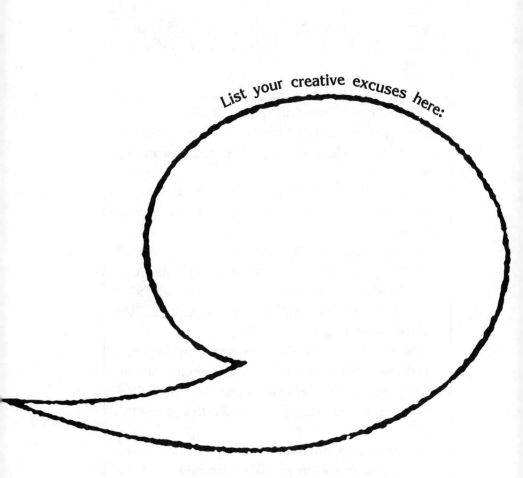

List your creative excuses here:

We all need an occasional whack on the side of the head to shake us out of routine patterns, to force us to rethink our problems, and to stimulate us to ask new questions that may lead to other right answers.

Roger von Oech, Author
A Whack On the Side of the Head

The Thrill Of The Hunt

Never learn to do anything: If you don't learn,
you'll always find someone else to do it for you.
—Mark Twain

Contrary to popular opinion, not all librarians are barbarians. Most of them are willing to help you, and you should cultivate their friendship. Indeed, they have the research keys to unlock the mysteries of most homework assignments.

All you have to do is learn to "borrow" the keys. Please consider these suggestions:

1. Act as if the librarians own the place. Pour on the compliments:

 Compare their magnificent library to the pitiful library at your former school where you were frustrated for so many years.

Show amazement at their skill in mastering this critical link in learning.

 Charmingly (and often) refer to your relative stupidity in these matters.

2. Avoid the Stanley Kowalski "I want it now" approach. This seldom succeeds unless you notice the librarian chewing on the card catalogue or relying on the kindness of strangers.

'I WANT IT NOW!!!'

Of course, manipulating librarians is just one method for gaining access to the library's "storehouse of knowledge." Here are some others:

 Phone former teachers who are both friendly with you and familiar with the library. (You'll be pleasantly surprised to find most are willing to assist.)

Study with someone who is library-wise and doesn't mind showing off her stuff in the stacks. Former and current debate team members are usually good people to know.

Hang around the reference books and ask someone who looks like he belongs there. Do not loiter by the Reader's Guide To Periodical Literature where every "dim bulb" goes. Be discriminating. Linger by the less trafficked areas; the Index Medicus or the Index to the Book Reviews in the Humanities.

Make sure that you begin your research with a plan. Do not be like Stephen Leacock's famous horseman and "ride off madly in all directions." You should think through all possible contingencies before they arrive or you will waste valuable time weeping on your Websters.

Being prepared with different approaches is imperative if you start your effort with information that is less than complete or is inaccurate. According to a pamphlet published by one college library, there are more than 800 cards separating "commission for" from "commission on" and "Paterson" files two drawers away from "Patterson." You can imagine the potential confusion caused by a handout typo or a teacher's scrawls on a blackboard.

When organizing a subject search, keep in mind that in order to avoid card catalogue chaos, words or phrases known as subject headings have been chosen to stand for all their synonyms. The standardized subject terminology is based on the books, *Library of Congress Subject Headings*, more popularly known as the Red Books.

 A word of caution from one librarian: The Red Books do not include the most recently approved terms. You can find cards in the catalogue under headings like Computer crimes, Embassy takeovers, City planning, Afro-Americans, Househusbands, and Trucking. But these are too new to be found in the Red Books. This means that you may have to follow up on certain terms just in case they have not yet been included.

 If you are interested in members of the opposite inclination, then take this opportunity to really make your time well-spent in the library. Pick the most attractive member of the other sex to ask a question of. Take a chance on the laws of probability.

 If all else fails, teach yourself to use the library. Fortunately, there is a book available to simplify this process. Alden Todd's *Finding Facts Fast* is the resource that you need. It is divided into sections for beginning, intermediate, and advanced researchers. For the beginner, Mr. Todd assumes you know nothing, and without condescension, and in very few pages to read, leads you to the land of library happiness.

So, happy hunting. In the library, too.

Writer's Block But Seldom Tackle

Let's face it, writing is hell.
—**William Styron**

Writer's block is traditionally defined as an obstacle to free expression of ideas on paper, but any student who has once faced a writing assignment can tell you that blockage is a way of life.

Clearly, being forced to think is a pain in the brain. Having to write using that same process merely adds insult to injury. We become vulnerable. We listen to the doubts of our internal critics: "This paper is second-rate rubbish!" or "You couldn't write your way out of a paper bag."

We experience the dread that our external critics, both teachers and peers, will agree with our derogatory assessment.

We procrastinate.

We begin to do crazy things to avoid completing the assignment. Counting holes in ceiling tile, tapping out tunes with a #2 pencil, looking up dirty words in the dictionary.

IT DOESN'T HAVE TO BE THE MOON.
JUST TAKE ME SOMEWHERE ELSE.

We sit down to the typewriter— "The quick brown fox..."

We sense the walls are slowly closing in. We open our mouths to scream, but there is absolute silence.

Each professional writer, like each student, confronts the reality of idea blockage. Oscar Wilde once claimed that he had spent the morning putting in a comma, and the afternoon taking it out again. F. Scott Fitzgerald found his solution in tap dancing. Brian Wilson (of the Beach Boys) placed his piano in a sandbox. A student we interviewed confessed that his best papers were formulated while sitting in the shower.

As you experiment with mind games (avoiding drugs and booze as options), we urge you to study the next section carefully for concrete suggestions on how to stimulate creative juices.

Random Thoughts

- Type (or if you're lucky enough to have access to a computer, word process) your papers. Handwritten papers with ruffled ridges will often cause even the best writing to be overlooked by a weary teacher.
- If you can't type, (1) learn, or (2) barter with a non-creative student who needs ideas (and doesn't have a copy of this book), or (3) find someone who is willing to type for you.
- Photocopy all of your papers. For a nickel a page (average cost) you can avoid the heart and brainache caused by the absent-minded professor who misplaces your Herculean effort and then claims you must have never turned it in. Just drop that photocopy on the desk and save the useless tears and idle threats.

Never Lose Interest In Borrowing

The past is but a beginning of a beginning.
—H.G. Wells

It was probably a hirsute graduate student, struggling to eke out an existence in some ancient academia who, while playing "mutton, mutton, who's got the mutton?" and idly carving a replica of his friend Ugg's new round invention into a nearby tree, first said:

COPYING ONE BOOK IS PLAGIARISM;
COPYING SEVERAL IS RESEARCH.

No matter, really, who originated the notion, suffice it to say, the idea caught on.

In discussing plagiarism, it is important to draw some distinctions. Material considered in the public domain or "common knowledge" is traditionally (according to those in the scholarly community) handled differently than material protected by copyright. One who gives credit, of course, is not plagiarizing.

It is not surprising, then, that when writers give credit to others for "influencing" their work, it is many times merely polite writer talk for explaining away their wholesale borrowing.

Most, but not all, authors will 'fess up to their filching. Woody Allen, in an interview with Dick Cavett, readily admitted to borrowing from S.J. Perelman and Robert Benchley; on the other hand, scholars are still debating the merits of Poe's savage attacks on Longfellow for aping European writers (and believe it or not, even the tender ballad, "Yes, We Have No Bananas" is strangely reminiscent of Handel's "Messiah").

History is replete with alarming accusations of literary larceny.

Do not be shocked. All writers borrow from the past—their past experiences combined with their knowledge of literary or scientific or inventive works of the past. The successful ones do it more creatively.

The key to creative production of any sort is creative thinking— you must make the associations between the work of others and your experiences.

This important principle was made clear to this author when I was a high school journalist. My assignment on our paper was to crank out a bi-weekly editorial. In the first issue, after extensive research and soul searching reflection, I strongly supported the thesis that my fellow students should refrain from cutting into the lunch line.

This was coupled with a scathing indictment of shoving in the hallways. In short, I failed to break much new ground in high school editorial land.

I DON'T THINK YOU UNDERSTOOD MY EDITORIAL. I ONLY MEANT THAT I HAD A BURNING DESIRE TO READ...

By comparison, a contemporary of mine wrote an editorial that compared the future of the high school student of 1966 to Shakespeare's "Seven Ages of Man."

"Hmmmmm . . ." I thought.

In the paper's second issue, my editorial could have been condensed into the admonition, "Let's all be friends."

My contemporary, in his column, penned a eulogy to a local second-grade teacher who had recently passed away. The structure of the editorial was a time-capsule trip back to a typical day in this teacher's classroom. Without sentimentality, and with extraordinary sensitivity, the editorial paid tribute to how this teacher had changed her students' lives.

After rereading and studying these editorials, it became painfully apparent to me that one of us was thinking creatively; and the other was not. One of us was applying the principle of "borrowing," and the other was stacking marshmallows in the wind.

I learned from this literary lesson—I suggest you do the same. Begin by experimenting with the following formats that will add flair to any written assignment.

Literary Lessons

The Recipe Paper

The ingredients for this approach include passages from ten to twenty published sources, all related, in some way, to the subject of your essay. You simply lift a well-written group of sentences from each source and record this information on notecards. Then paraphrase (rewriting with as much imagination as possible) each notecard's contents on to a new notecard. Next, lay your cards on a table, read them aloud, over and over, until a common theme becomes evident. (Note: Not all cards will fit into any given theme. Be selective.) This common idea that you have discovered should be developed into a thesis statement (see page 101).

Now choose one of the most compelling cards. (This means that when you read it your reaction is, "Golly that is amazing!") This statement becomes the introduction to your essay.

Finally, you place the remainder of the cards in their most logical sequence. Drop the irrelevant ones and group them into two or three major issues that explain or support the thesis.

All that's left for you to do is to write transitional statements linking the cards together and to add a finish to the paper (see pages 101 – 103 for a complete example).

The No Analysis Necessary Paper

This approach is used when you are required to write about a subject on which you have no previous knowledge. Or on a subject which is far too complicated for the limited time you have to complete the assignment.

Variation 1

A student taking an education class was asked to compare the ideas of Malcom X to the "organic" teaching method of author Silvia Ashton-Warner. She decided to write an imaginary dialogue between Ms. Ashton-Warner and Malcom X as if they were teacher and young student. No original thought was necessary because all of the lines were taken directly from published works by Ms. Ashton-Warner and Malcom X.

By simply matching lines from books, this student received an A+ on the paper. And she never had to directly address the complex challenge inherent in the assignment.

Variation 2

If you are asked to review a performance of a play like Samuel Beckett's *Waiting for Godot* there is still hope.

A possible strategy in this case is not to review the play itself but the audience. During intermission and following the performance, carefully listen to the comments of audience members and record their mini-reviews. Some may even be willing to be interviewed more extensively after the performance or the next day by phone. Take all of your recorded responses and group them into categories.

Next, lift lines from the text of the play to use as introductory passages to those categories you've selected. For example, if you really did have to review *Waiting For Godot*, your three category headings might be based on the "anticipation," the "waiting," and the "disappointment." Just plug in the audience comments under the appropriate heading and write transitions.

Variation 3

For certain topics the "Martian" approach may be effective. Let us say you were assigned to write a paper titled "Can the United Nations Ever Achieve World Peace?"

You write a first-person narrative as if you were a visitor from another planet. Naturally, you as an extraterrestrial and you as a student know nothing about international relations. How convenient for the both of you.

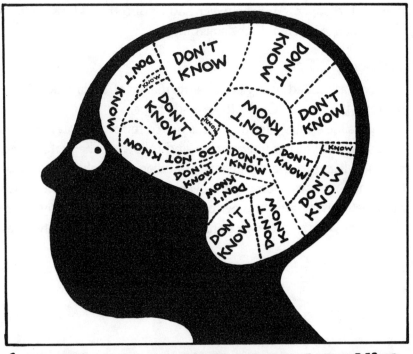

'MY, MY, THE THINGS THAT I DON'T KNOW WOULD FILL A BOOK!'

The Recycling Papers Gambit

If and when you finally write a first-rate paper, you should try to capitalize on your effort as soon as possible. Try to persuade your teachers to allow you to shift their assigned topics to a topic that you have "always wanted to research." Or, if that doesn't work, ask if you can turn in a paper for extra credit; of course you forget to mention your paper was originally written for another class. (Some students we've talked to have essays that have seen more miles than Robert Frost, and more A's than banana.) Be sure to see if your school has any rules prohibiting recycling papers. If it is not permitted, take a pass on this option.

Paper Train Yourself

As we pointed out in an earlier chapter, teachers are human beings, too. They have the same fervency for the frivolous, the same driving desire to bandy about boisterous badinage. After all, would you like to read and evaluate thirty essays on the lighter side of *Paradise Lost?*

Creative students take advantage of the weakness in the old academic armor. They clothe their content in structures that are tailor-made to tickle a teacher's fancy.

Here are four more structural approaches which students have found successful:

Ordinary Poople

It is often a wise strategy to let the teacher know you can read. And although using a literary device is not that original it is almost always a safe choice.

 A familiar passage from Shakespeare is adapted to create a vehicle for an essay on fear.

"All the world's a stage,
    And all the men and women merely players,
    And one man in his time plays many parts,
    His acts being seven ages."

These words from the pen of William Shakespeare, in his work *As You Like It,* remind us so vividly of the transience of life.

When Shakespeare wrote those famous lines, he could never have imagined how many of the players would someday suffer from stage fright. For them the stage—the world—is a fearful place.

W.H. Auden described this time in history as an "age of anxiety." Albert Camus called it the "century of fear." For indeed, according to the Health Institute of New York, some 18 million Americans are victims of irrational, persistent fears.

One out of every 12 of us is debilitated by these fears, and whether you realize it or not, the rest of us are adversely affected. Therefore, we must learn to control our fears, or most certainly, they will control us. Let us begin in the beginning.

"At first the infant, mewling and puking in the nurse's arms."

The psychologists' debate over an infant's "original" fears may never be settled . . .

Katherine, 15

The novel *Silas Marner* is adapted to create a vehicle for an essay on the sale of infant formula to the Third World.

"...The heap of gold seemed to glow and get larger beneath his agitated gaze. He stretched forth his hand, but instead of the hard coin, his fingers encountered soft, warm curls."

Silas Marner was a secluded misanthrope, a nearsighted, narrow-minded miser who missed only his gold, but, by providence, mistook a child for his fortune and became a man again.

Unfortunately for us, such misers as Silas Marner still thrive today, near-sighted multinationals who see the glittering gold in every child and nothing more.

Tom, 16

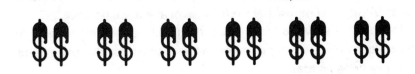

Talk'n Role

The key to developing this vehicle is for the first person narrator to assume a fictional role.

 In writing a paper on the jury system in America, the narrator pretends to be a prosecutor placing that system on trial.

May it please the court. As prosecuting attorney in the case of *justice v. the jury system,* I am here today to prove to you, once and for all, that the jury system truly is an inadequate measure of justice.

Case in point: Pat Powis, a middle-aged San Francisco secretary, was asked to serve on jury duty in the Dan White murder case. She convinced the rest of the jurors, that Dan White, who was seen killing the mayor of San Francisco, was not guilty. Pat's reasoning was that White, a former police chief, was unaware that murder was illegal.

Case in point: Edward Simpson, occupation unknown, was charged with rape in the case of Simpson v. The State of Utah. After a six month trial, he was found innocent because the jury failed to reach a unanimous verdict.

Eleven jurors voted "guilty," one voted "not guilty." As Mr. Simpson was leaving the courtroom, the one unyielding juror approached him and said, "We let you go this time, but don't do it again."

It seems the victim of this rape was raped twice: Once by Mr. Simpson, and once by our system of justice.

Implicit in these and hundreds of other examples is the belief that the jury system is not working. Ordinary citizens are simply not capable of or, in some instances, willing to do the job. Perhaps Herbert Spencer was right: "A jury is composed of twelve men of average ignorance."

We must all strive to make jurors both willing and able to serve jury duty. Until we do, it is time, ladies and gentlemen, for the jury system in America to go on trial.

Preeta, 16

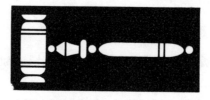

In this passage, the narrator tries to convince us that she is working for the famous cartoonist Charles Schulz. Please note how cleverly she shifts into a persuasive paper on the treatment of the elderly.

Good afternoon, my name is Katie Johnson. I have been hired to represent Charles Monroe Schulz. I'm sure most of you know that Mr. Schulz is the creator of the comic strip "Peanuts." As his representative, I've been asked to inform you that beginning Monday, "Peanuts" will no longer be published. Mr. Schulz is deeply saddened by his decision, but because he has always prided himself in being an "onbeat" cartoonist, he feels it is necessary.

Mr. Schulz believes that "Peanuts" is no longer "onbeat." A comic strip that once focused on the cruelty that exists between children now seems strangely irrelevant (offbeat.)

Mr. Schulz made his difficult decision when he learned that today one out of nine people are 65 years or older, and shortly after the turn of the century that ratio will have increased to one out of six. And already 30% of the aged live in substandard housing, 20% live in poverty, and 86% have chronic health problems. These depressing statistics have become increasingly haunting, increasingly "onbeat" as Mr. Schulz approaches his own retirement.

Katie, 17

This narrator, in the tradition of Jonathan Swift and Mark Twain, has written a mock encomium, a form of satire in which pretended praise is actually blame. Incidentally, the paper from which this passage was taken received second place in the National Scholastic Writing Awards Contest.

I'm not crazy! I'm in touch with heaven. And it don't matter what you think 'cause I'm on my way to heaven. The Lord is with me. I know 'cause I got a personal message from the Lord while watching Reverend Pat Robertson on the 700 Club. I was revelated through the Kingdom Principles and the word of knowledge. You know, I can still remember Rev. Robertson saying, "I have a word of knowledge." And he said, "There is a lady in Kansas City who has sinus. The Lord is drying up that sinus right now. Thank you Jesus. And there is a lady in Cincinnati with cancer of the lymph nodes. Well, I don't know if it's been diagnosed yet, but she hasn't been feelin' very well. But the Lord is dissolving the cancer right now. Thank you Jesus." And then, Rev. Robertson spoke right to me and he said, "My friends, there is a young lady in Lincoln, Nebraska, who can become a prophet for the Lord."

Sue, 16

More Ideas:

- A paper written by Tom Sawyer set in the current year.
- An imaginary sequel to *Babbitt* in which Ted Babbitt (the son) discusses how his views on materialism changed during the depression.
- A mock encomium treatment of military recruiting practices.

Arts 'n Crafty

These methods require throwing away your preconceived notions of essay form. The writing effort is usually more intellectually demanding and, thus, more time consuming.

 This oration (which could have easily been an essay assignment) was written as a play. The following excerpt demonstrates how the content was integrated into theatrical conventions.

The title of my oration is "It Is Greater To Be Human," a sadly human play about us. Our play is in three acts.

Act I

The curtain rises on the playground of life. Suddenly a child finds himself lifted from his mother's embrace and plopped into kindergarten, where each assignment is carefully graded, indicating to the child the exact amount of approval his performance has been awarded. His popularity with teachers and students is contingent upon his degree of success.

"What did you learn in school today, dear little boy of mine? What did you learn in school today?"

"Our team's behind in the money race. Only four kids brought their money for the magazine subscriptions."

"My team won the baseball spelling game. I got three hits and one out. I misspelled goat."

Val, 17

In this passage you will see how the idea of "making a difference in other people's lives" became an essay turned poem. This is perhaps the most challenging of approaches because so few young people, anymore, are versed in verses.

Take note that the student author has taken lines from e e cummings' work to introduce the reader to the poet's philosophy of life. Then, after the thesis statement (you, too, should make a difference), the author begins his version of cummings, famous poem, "anyone lived in a pretty how town." The final two lines illustrate how you can place original content in a borrowed structure.

It's no use trying to pretend that most people and ourselves are alike. You and I are human beings; most people are snobs. Take the matter of being born. What does being born mean to most people? Catastrophe unmitigated...you and I are not snobs. We can never be born enough. We are human beings for whom birth is a supremely welcome mystery; The mystery of growing; The mystery which happens only and whenever we are faithful to ourselves. You and I wear the dangerous looseness of doom and find it becoming. Life, for eternal us, is now...

edward estlin cummings was never especially impressed by the heroics of the people convinced that they are about to change the world. He was more awed by the heroics of those who are willing to struggle to make one small difference after another.

In tribute to and in memory of Mr. cummings and anyone — I want to persuade you that you, too, should make a difference.

A Poem For Anyone

Anyone lived in pretty condominium
with upstairs neighbors and privacy at a minium...

Craig, 17

This is a fun approach for the writer fortunate enough to have a teacher with an off-the-wall sense of humor. The idea is to begin your writing assignment with a lie. Then, you cleverly shift to the true subject of your work.

Abortion

I believe in the "Right To Life." I believe that all people must have the opportunity to grow and to create. And yet, I believe in abortion. Yes, abortion. If we are to live, to grow and create, then we must have a-bore-tion. We must shun bores. We must ostracize these boring people. Yes, I believe in A-Bore-Shun.

A-BOAR-SHUN

If you use any of these approaches it is unlikely that you will be shunned by your teachers as a bore. Admittedly, these creative vehicles may not, in themselves, change your life. But they do have the potential to change your grades.

Somebody's boring me . . . I think it's me.

— *Dylan Thomas*

You Can Have Your Cake And Edit, Too

All of us learn to write in the second grade. . .
most of us go on to greater things.

— Bobby Knight

Recent research in language has revealed that English teachers prefer muddy, verbose writing to clear, simple writing. Syndicated columnist Charles McCabe, summarized these new studies and pointed out that "Even people who can write good English prefer to write the pompous brand that so conned their teachers and continues to con their superiors and clients."

Therefore, we recommend two courses of action.

1. Spend an evening of heavy page petting and mental caressing with Strunk and White's *Elements of Style*. Make sure that the seeds of knowledge are firmly planted in your mind. This book is easy, particularly when compared to other forms of social intercourse.

2. Add flair to the fundamentals by using "literary spicers."

Alliteration

the repetition of consonants, especially at the beginning of words or stressed syllables.

Diversionary psychology, that marvelous new idea mesmerizing millions of Americans, that super new subject selling stacks and stacks of psychologically sensible suggestions in the blazing beauty of brilliantly bound books.

Sex sells, and almost everyone buys. From prepubescent Pollyannas with money more and mind less to the brightest of brights. Certainly adults have the right to purchase the promise of perfect pleasure, be it Playboy bunnies or plastic paraphernalia; but we must also pursue realistic expectations.

parallel phrasing

repetition in structure which combines similar form and length in word choice.

If we accept the reality of our fears, rather than avoiding them, and if we act realistically to face our fears rather than destructively to deny them, then and only then, we will be at peace when we reach retirement.

Lactogen is neither a disease nor a germ but a brand name. A heavily promoted and popular product in the third world, pushed as modernity at the loss of maternity, mortality and morbidity at the loss of mother's milk. (In this example both alliteration and parallel phrasing are used.)

Similes and **Metaphors**

A simile is an expressed comparison between two essentially different items using a term such as "like" or "as." A metaphor includes a word which in ordinary usage signifies one kind of thing, quality, or action, now applied to another, without expressed indication of a relation between them.

Examples:

A classic example of a simile is poet Robert Burn's "O my love's like a red, red rose." However, we could change the line into a metaphor as follows, "O my love is a red, red rose."

Here is another metaphor as it might be expanded in an essay on greed:

Little and big, our society is one of piggies. We are simply far too concerned with only ourselves. Most of us pass our days in isolated barnyards, wallowing in self-pity, dragging others through the mud, growing fatter until it just doesn't matter, snorting about this, sniveling about that...and never giving one generous "oink" for our neighbor pig.

Clever WORDPLAY

→ The thrill of popularity, the agony of not being neat.

→ A young man is told: "In relationships it's not success; it's sexcess and in excess. It's not how meaningful; it's how many fall and in double standard time.

→ Over prescription: When a hippocratic oaf prescribes too much of a drug.

Examples:

→ The subversive nature of the intellectual portion of our society also presents an enormous threat to our national well-being. With the sole exception of the Great Poultry Revolt of 1842 (known as the Chicken Coup) the eggheads have been the first to be jailed in any insurrection.

This example ties together Tennessee Williams' early plays with his recent pannings by the critics:

With each new opening, a crass menagerie of critics urge Mr. Williams to take that one last ride on a streetcar named retire.

Clearly, the literary spicers provided in this section are just a sample of what can be done. Remember, though, very few of your classmates will make the effort to add these creative and compelling touches to their work. If you can sacrifice the time and endure the mental strain needed to spice up your papers, your work will increase in quality. Plus, many teachers will be so impressed by these flourishes that they will forgive some of the other weaknesses in your writings.

> **One moment of sublimity in a work of faults**
> **is better than consistent mediocrity.**
> — *Longinus*

Ver-bull-izing

The road to good grades is paved
with 'bull' dozing.
— **R. McCutcheon**

In my checkered (but few checks) career as an actor, freelance advertising copywriter, radio announcer, television movie reviewer, college and high school teacher, I have learned that the ability to communicate effectively is an invaluable skill for a lazy person — or, as my grandfather would say:

"Yep, I was in the Battle of Bull Run.
I shot the bull and it's still running."

Sadly, for you speech purists out there, my grandfather had a firm grasp on rhetorical reality. The hallowed halls of the honor roll are crowded with students who have discovered this principle of sound over substance. A principle that means many times, "It's not what you say but how you say it" that matters.

Demosthenes, an oratorical oldie but goodie, was once asked what was the most important canon of rhetoric. He replied, "Delivery." To a second inquiry, he replied, "Delivery." And when asked a third time he answered, "Delivery." Well, you get the idea.

Politicians have fashioned careers around this self-evident truth. A classic example of how this process works is included in *The Book of Lists 2* by David Wallechinsky, Irving Wallace, Amy Wallace and Sylvia Wallace.

Claude Pepper v. George Smathers
U.S. Senatorial Primary Election (1950)

At the start of the McCarthy era, Floridian Claude Pepper, one of the Senate's most outspoken liberals, was on the conservative's "hit list" along with many other senators. George Smathers lashed out with some typical right-wing invective. He called his opponent "The Red Pepper," and he launched a campaign to expose Pepper's secret "vices." Smathers disclosed that Pepper was a known "extrovert," his sister was a "thespian," and his brother a "practicing homo-sapien." Also, when Pepper went to college, he actually "matriculated." Worst of all, he practiced "celibacy" before marriage. Naturally, rural voters were horrified, and Pepper lost.

'MY MEALY-MOUTHED OPPONENT IS A WELL-KNOWN MASTICATOR!'

From this black day in campaign history it is clear that "Mr. Pepper," like the "Doctor" of the same name, was so misunderstood. It should also be apparent by now, even to the uninitiated, that the students who are skilled in speech have a distinct advantage over their silent partners in class. If oral discussions are counted as a factor in grading, then that advantage takes on increased importance.

We recommend that students force themselves to speak during class discussions. Do not argue that it doesn't make that much difference, that you don't know what to say, or that you are afraid to talk. Those are excuses, not valid arguments. If it's any consolation, here's what students have to say about speaking up in class:

"I always think, 'How stupid am I going to be if I ask this question?' But you have to ask or you suffer."

Ken, 18

"Just think, you might be helping someone else out by asking your question."

Matt, 17

You must learn to speak in front of others if you want to make full measure of your potential. Denying the reality of your plight is futile rationalization. The point is moot, or should we say, mute.

Here are some suggestions for overcoming the fear of ver-bull-izing.

The laugh track might have responded favorably, but ignore the "Brady Bunch" advice to imagine the audience sitting out there in nothing but their underwear. This solution loses all psychological persuasiveness within a few seconds after what could have only been a disgusting mental picture.

Staring at the foreheads or over the heads of the audience (or out the window or at a wall) becomes disconcerting to listeners, even if they're not sure why. This lack of direct eye contact may be comforting to the speaker, but audience members are left feeling strangely uneasy. Instead, experiment with the following two techniques. They have been used with great success by speech students even when under the pressure of interscholastic competition.

Grin like a monkey. For most people, smiling confidently and being nervous are incompatible physiological responses. With the exception of those few who giggle and turn silly in anxiety, this approach of smiling when confronting the symptoms of fear is immediately calming. The trick is to force yourself to smile the instant you recognize the symptoms.

I'LL GRIN BUT I REFUSE TO BARE ANYTHING.

Instant Jokes — The split-second you are aware of your anxiety, you should say a "one-liner" (to yourself). Then, quickly refocus your attention on the subject of your speech. Here are some sample one-liners:

You feel drops of sweat pouring from your armpits and staining your shirt. You instantly say to yourself, "Great! I won't need to take a bath this week." Immediately after, you must return your full attention to the content of your speech.

You are certain that your heart is pounding so loudly that people in the back row are quaking from the vibrations. Using the same basic process as before, you say, "Hooray, maybe someone will finally ask me to dance."

Your voice cracks and you say to yourself, "Wow, at last I am going to pass through puberty."

In each case, the important step is to shift your concentration back to the speech right after you have made your "instant joke."

These techniques are designed to ease you through those periods of oral panic. They will not, however, help you in knowing what to say. Clearly it is impossible (and probably not desirable) for us to put words in your mouth.

Each class will demand different techniques. Each student comes with a different background. As a rule, however, if you are timid about talking in class, you should begin with some simple statements or questions:

"May I get a drink of water?"

"Would you please repeat what you just said?"

"Is a nod as good as a wink to a blind horse?"

Here are some more serious guidelines to observe in deciding when and what to ask of your teacher. If you can offer a constructive opinion, provide some new information, or support the discussion of a classmate, then you can be certain your observation is appropriate.

Now we realize it is extremely difficult for some students to overcome natural shyness. Often a reluctance to speak up in class is rooted in the fear of being thought of as "weird" or "looking like a fool."

To overcome this difficulty we suggest these two strategies:

- Summarize and tie together the unrelated points your classmates have been making. This makes it easier for you to generate relevant discussion and get answers to questions that will fill holes in everyone's gaps of information.

- Prepare a few questions the night before class and practice saying them over and over.

The key to building confidence in your ability to speak in class is to start listening carefully to what other students say. Remember the 3 R's of effective discussion. Your comments should be relevant, reliable and respectful. At the same time you should avoid being redundant.

Students who wish to reap the benefits of having more fun in class and better grades through ver-bull-izing will progress to whole paragraphs of public speaking. And from there to contributing serious content to class discussions.

Remember, for the lazy student, talk is cheap. But silence is oh-so costly.

This Is Only A Test

Do you happen to know how many tassels a Restoration Coxcomb wore at the knee? Or the kind of chafing dish a bunch of Skidmore girls would have used in a dormitory revel in 1911? Or the exact method of quarrying peat out of a bog at the time of the Irish Corn Laws? In fact, do you know anything at all that nobody else knows or, for that matter, gives a damn about?

—S.J. Perelman

In freshman English, my professor would refer to us, collectively, as those happy hicks from "huskerland" or those *#!!@* rubes from the farm, which seemed all right at the time, since he was usually plowed. Between epithets of encouragement, however, he did make one observation which I have found a valuable insight into successful test-taking.

It's Not How Much
You Know That Counts,
But How Well You Use
What You Do Know.

If you want to be "in the know," especially at test-taking times, we suggest the following:

1 Take comfort that you are not alone in the world of "temporary test trauma." Consider these examples of lazy students:

Thomas A. Edison, U.S. Inventor

Edison's peculiar inquisitiveness as a young child impressed nobody but his tolerant mother. His first teacher described him as "addled," his father almost convinced him he was a "dunce," and his headmasters warned that he "would never make a success of anything." Under his mother's tutelage, however, Edison became a precocious reader; and he was soon making practical inventions. He eventually patented over a thousand inventions whose worth to humankind is incalculable.

Giacomo Puccini, Italian Opera Composer

The creator of *Tosca, La Boheme,* and *Madame But-terfly* was born into a family of church musicians and was expected to follow the tradition. However, he was utterly unambitious. He did poorly in school and even caused his first music teacher to give up in despair, concluding that he had no talent. Fortunately, the approach of his second music teacher caught his fancy; and from that moment Puccini energetically devoted himself to music.

2

Fortunately for you, few tests require that you do much thinking. Despite continuing efforts to reform testing procedures, few changes have been made in the classroom. It is not surprising then, that the Educational Testing Service concluded that the ways materials are taught in classrooms haven't progressed much in 25 years either.

What this means for you is that your achievement is still measured by your ability to memorize massive amounts of largely irrelevant information. Therefore, if you choose to make the best of a bad situation, refine your cramming techniques.

Initially, you need to be very selective about what you try to remember. Force yourself to choose only the most important elements that were covered in class. Drill on those items. If you attempt to memorize all of the material, your brain will probably malfunction from overload. Take a gamble on your judgement and drill, drill, drill. Recite aloud the important elements over and over and over and over and over again. Make use of mnemonic devices such as these offered by students in an advanced chemistry class:

Leo says ger (i.e. Loss of electrons is oxidation
Gain of electrons is reduction)

Roy G. Biv (i.e. the colors of the spectrum:
Red, orange, yellow, green, blue, indigo and violet)

Remember the story of "SOH-CAH-TOA"?

$$\text{Sin} \angle = \frac{\text{Opposite side}}{\text{Hypotenuse}}$$

$$\text{Cos} \angle = \frac{\text{Adjacent side}}{\text{Hypotenuse}}$$

$$\text{Tan} \angle = \frac{\text{Opposite side}}{\text{Adjacent side}}$$

If you are conscientious in your drilling, then you will benefit from the "Vaccination Theory of Education." Neil Postman and Charles Weingartner, authors of *Teaching as a Subversive Activity*, used this theory to explain how once students have taken a course and passed the test, they are "immune" and will never again have to demonstrate any real learning in that subject.

3 Most teachers talk at a rate of about 100 words per minute. Believe it or not, you are able to think about four times that fast. Use that "extra" time to make sense of what is being said. Do that and you will significantly reduce the need for long hours of studying later.

4 Richard P. Gallagher, an educational consultant in Pennsylvania, recommends that you take notes only on the right-hand half of the notebook pages. Save the other half for your own comments and teachers questions. Mr. Gallagher is on to something. Teachers are constantly giving clues to potential test questions by repeating a fact several times, by writing it on the board, or by subtly saying it will be on an upcoming exam.

5 When you are reviewing for a test, be sure to take many breaks. After an hour or two of studying, people reach a point of diminishing returns. Pushing beyond your natural limits will not increase learning; it will merely decrease desire. The quality of study time is the critical factor in being adequately prepared. Therefore, study the most difficult subjects first while you are most alert.

6 Pay attention to directions. On short-answer and essay questions it is imperative that you figure out precisely what the question is asking. The exact wording of what is asked should dictate your answer. Key words in the questions will guide you. There is a difference, for example, between the verbs "compare" and "contrast." To "enumerate" is not to "analyze." However, the ambiguous "discuss" can be interpreted to mean: compare, contrast, enumerate, analyze, explain, defend, describe, etc.

7 Write neatly, be brief, and be clear. (Pencil is a pain to read according to most teachers, so always use a pen.) Grading short answer and essay questions can be largely a subjective exercise. Don't give a "burned-out" teacher a reason to take out frustrations on you.

8 Do not form a "study group" unless you plan to study. Otherwise, you end up with a social group that gets together to avoid the loneliness of *not* learning.

9 There is a little book, a mere 75 pages, that can greatly improve your test-taking skills. *Test-Wiseness* was developed by the American College and is published by McGraw-Hill. It is sometimes difficult to track down, so it may be necessary for you to get it through interlibrary loan.

10 In each class, always attempt to find old tests that were given by the same teacher. Most teachers are ambitious enough to continually create new questions, but there will always be patterns that you can decipher. For example, in true-false questions, does your teacher consistently favor one over the other. In multiple choice does she favor particular letters or use sentence patterns that are giveaways?

Closely examine not only the type of essay questions that the teacher asks, but how this instructor evaluates the answers. Is more value given to content or form? How does he react to creative approaches? Can you expect "trick" questions?

In short, studying old tests might be the most efficient use of your midnight oil.

In times of quiet desperation, when you suddenly realize that you are facing a major exam, and you have no idea how to prepare, pay a visit to the teacher. You would be surprised how much valuable information can be acquired if you are both direct and tactful.

One student we talked with demonstrated the good that can come of such a visit.

He was dismayed to discover that his semester grade in "Introduction to Political Science" would be determined by only two hour long exams and a final. Following a D+ on the first exam, and a B− on the second, dismay turned to depression. At the last moment, reason triumphed over reluctance and he set up an appointment with the professor.

The conversation went something like this: "I have always been an A student. But in your class I have been disappointed with myself. I have worked very hard (expecting lightning to strike) but evidently in vain."

"I do not want any special favors...I am willing to do all the work, but could you give me some ideas on what to study for the final?"

YOU MAY NOT BELIEVE THIS, BUT I AM WORRIED ABOUT MY GRADE...

The professor then handed him a sheet of paper that contained a list of ten questions. She informed him that the three questions on the final would be taken from the list.

Twelve hours later, the student had memorized ten compelling arguments with specific supporting material for each question.

Fortunately, he didn't blank out the next morning. He scored an A+ on the final and received an A in the course.

It is important to note that not all teachers will help in this way. Not all would have given the benefit of the doubt when it came to final grades. But what if this student, for fear of rejection, hadn't asked?

12 When answering essay test questions, you will have greater success if you follow a specific structural approach. The form that follows is widely used by public speakers. We've provided you a complete example to give you a model to follow. We've also annotated each section with an explanation of each necessary element. (This essay was written by a high school student in less than thirty minutes.)

Essay question: How will Margaret Thatcher change Britain?

(Please note that the right side explanations are for instructional purposes only and were obviously not included in the test answer.)

Britain's socialism was at its finest recently when the department of trade, taking off the top a small number of box receipts, decided to give money to cultural classics such as Erotic Inferno, The Playbirds, and Let's Get Naughty.

Certainly, it seemed to many British people that perhaps socialism was going just a bit too far. And that the labor government sponsoring socialism, the power of the unions, and other things that people didn't like was going too far. So far that change was required, a change that brought us to the conservative party and Margaret Thatcher.

It is not surprising then, that many people were asking what other changes were in store and asking the question, "How will Margaret Thatcher change Britain?" The answer is very simple. She will make a move toward conservatism, less involvement by government, and less power for the unions.

But in order to understand my position, we must take three perspectives.

Initially, we will examine Thatcher's economic policies, then her policies on union power, and finally, the most emotional issue, her policies on immigration.

Margaret Thatcher recently characterized herself as wanting a radical departure from the socialism that has pervaded Britain in the last few years. Prime Minister Callahan puts it differently; he says that she will "slaughter" the democratic and socialist programs which he feels have been the basis for a strong Britain.

One thing is certain, however, Britain's economy has been failing; and no one is certain why.

Paul Samuelson, the economist, notes that Britain's growth rate has suffered so much over the last ten years that it has lagged far behind the United States and European countries. He notes that Margaret Thatcher, therefore, is going to attempt to slash the tax rate that is considered both regressive and repressive for investors in Britain. There is a 98% maximum tax rate. Furthermore, she is looking for massive cuts in government spending. Yet, she has promised not to cut the sacred cows: Socialized medicine, education and pension funds.

The result, according to Mr. Samuelson, should not be a miracle. Perhaps, Mrs. Thatcher is looking for what Werner Erhardt found in 1949 when he cut, and then eliminated, all price controls in Germany. Subsequently, he was faced with a massive increase in economic structures and benefits. Samuelson notes that recent departures from socialism have not resulted in these panaceas. Mrs. Thatcher can expect similar consequences.

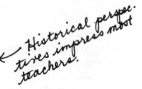
Historical perspectives impress most teachers.

However, that is but a small picture of Margaret Thatcher's policies — there is also a widespread influence that surprisingly enough is not the government, and that is the "unions."

Transition from first to second issue.

Columnist George F. Will pointed out that in a recent survey Callahan rated a sad second to the "unions" as the most powerful influence in Britain. Bumper stickers appeared and said, "Vote for the unions and avoid the middle man." And it is conceded by most people that they control all power.

Use of humor adds variety and also rekindles interest for the reader.

Margaret Thatcher with her teacup-smashing style is likely to try to smash the "unions." Unfortunately for her, that may make things worse. Five million workers are up for renegotiations of their contracts this year and many Britainers feel that the "unions" know that she hates them, so they'll hate her as well. They won't want to renegotiate with her.

Notice effective use of language (e.g. "teacup smashing style.")

Mrs. Thatcher, though, does have specific proposals. First, she is trying to change the closed shop rules which keep a worker from working unless he joins the union. She wants court compensation for those who are fired. Secondly, she wants to change the rules regarding strikers and whether or not they receive pay. Mrs. Thatcher doesn't believe that they should. And finally, Mrs. Thatcher desires to bring about a decrease in "union" power; however, as with the economy any quick cures are not likely (for "unions" have been in power as long as anyone can remember).

Listing specific proposals adds content to essay & is a strong strategic move.

Clearly, the economy and the "unions" do not seem to be changing. One thing that Mrs. Thatcher is likely to change, though, is the immigration policy.

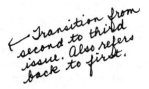
Transition from second to third issue. Also refers back to first.

Right now, anyone who comes from Eastern Asia is characterized as "Black" by those of British faith. And those Britainers also feel that racism is on the increase. For example, Margaret Thatcher stated in a news release that when the immigrants get to such a point that they begin to scare the people, then we should cut down on the immigrants.

This insight isn't common knowledge. a compelling choice to use in an essay

She does not point out, as "New Republic" reports that they only account for 4% of the total population in Britain. Hardly enough to scare many people.

But Margaret Thatcher knows that what works for racists works for her. Thus, the most emotional issue may also be the issue that Mrs. Thatcher will change most.

So in the final analysis, in looking at her changes, we see that Mrs. Thatcher is definitely moving toward conservatism.

And it does seem clear that the Labor Party was never one of only blue movies; but in analyzing the Labor Party, most Britainers saw red-programs, black immigrants, and yellow officials.

Clearly a change is coming. For as a tombstone in Britain recently read, "I told you I was sick." It is certain that Great Britain, too, has been sick for years. Now, it is up to Margaret Thatcher to cure the ailing economy before the nation dies.

Now that you have finished studying this annotated example, here is a sample examination question to test your mettle, as well as your mental abilities:

Q A man is walking down a road at four miles per hour. Another man is perfectly motionless but is holding five apples and four oranges. If gravity equals seriousness, and "x" is the 24th letter of the alphabet, then how much wood can a woodchuck chuck?

A

If you failed to answer, "As much wood as a woodchuck could chuck if a woodchuck could chuck wood," then you are easily distracted by extraneous information. We suggest you reread this chapter.

Supply-Side Theory

> The tools I need for my trade are paper,
> tobacco, food, and a little whiskey.
> — **William Faulkner**

With the rapidly escalating costs of a college education, many students need to find ways to cut corners in their financial planning. This chapter includes a few suggestions for reducing expenditures as well as a list of those "tools of the trade" that are worth every penny.

• Sell your old tests — charge the price of photocopying plus what the market will allow (keep all originals to be sold again the next semester). Timing is critical in selling old exams; the closer the date of doom, the higher the price. Remind your customers of the penalties for essay question plagiarism and require them to sign a contract guaranteeing ethical practices. Make them sign or don't sell. At all costs be certain that the buyer has only the honorable intention of purchasing a study aid.

- Don't buy books that are in the library. Go to the bookstore a few days early, find out the required texts, and then in collaboration with a classmate take turns checking the books out of the library so that they never revisit the shelves. Don't forget that the city libraries will often have some of the books too.

- Read assignments in the bookstore. As a junior in college, I purchased none of the books that were required for my courses. Instead, I would stand, as inconspicuously as possible, and pursue the reading assignments right there in the aisles. I don't recommend this for everyone, but it is possible.

IT'S SO HARD TO FIND A BOOKSTORE AISLE WITH A VIEW.

Tools Of The Trade

The following supplies are musts for a lazy student's survival:

Finding Facts Fast, Alden Todd. (Contains research techniques made understandable)

The Elements of Style, Strunk and White. (The best book on this subject and under 100 pages)

Peters Quotations, Dr. Laurence J. Peter. (Contemporary, complete. A simple way to give papers punch)

Word Watcher's Handbook, Phyllis Martin. (A Deletionary of the Most Abused and Misused Words)

Roget's International Thesaurus

A dictionary

The Kersten Brothers Catalog of Greeting Cards. (For creative correspondence—both academic and romantic) P.O. Box 5510, Scottsdale, AZ 85261

Time Rarely Flies

It is better to have loafed and lost
than never to have loafed at all.
—James Thurber

A high school principal once advised me that upon entering the "real world" I should spend eight minutes on each personal appointment. His theory was that any less than eight minutes and the person I was meeting with would feel slighted. Any more than eight minutes would only mean that nothing else would be accomplished. I then intimated that class periods be scheduled to last eight minutes. I was surreptitiously chastized for missing the point.

Which brings us to the point of this chapter...

When budgeting your time, the more selfish you are, the happier you are. But remember that in your attempts to be selfish, you will eventually fall prey to procrastination. This is an understandable behavior pattern when confronted by what W.S. Javons characterized as the "irksomeness" of work.

However, there are techniques that you can try to overcome this procrastination paralysis. These are just a few techniques recommended by Robert D. Rutherford, author of *Just In Time*.

Divide and Conquer

Take what seems to be an insurmountable task and divide it into more workable parts. Writing a book of 300 pages can seem an overwhelming task. But if you divide the work into manageable parts and write 400 carefully chosen words a day, you'll have yourself a book in just six months. This concept, applied to the limited nature of daily assignments, will make them seem much less formidable.

Start With A Part That Is Believable

If you are reluctant to do something because it is too large to take on, seems too difficult, or because you feel you cannot do it, select a part of the activity that you think is possible to complete. The old momentum theory will carry you on to tackle the rest of the project.

Make It Ridiculous

If the task is tedious or seemingly unrewarding, exaggerate the completion of the project in a way that is laughable. For example, can you imagine your teacher waiting breathlessly for the assignment with a wheelbarrow full of $1,000 bills upon its completion?

Reward Yourself Big

Choose a part of a task that you have been putting off. Make the reward for completing that part so great (or the penalty so severe) that you have no other option than to do the task. A typical reward might be sleeping in an hour or two when you'd normally force yourself to rise and shine. Remember, think big!

David and Goliath It

With this technique you simply face the problem squarely. There are going to be really tough assignments you just don't want to do. These are easily delayed. Nevertheless, they must be done. So— David and Goliath them. See yourself as battling an unpleasant, obnoxious, and obstinate giant. By defeating your imagined giant, you will feel the triumphant vibrations of victory. Or maybe just slingshot whiplash. (But it's worth a try anyway.)

Finally, in preparing to portion your life away, first schedule in a few hours to do nothing. Next, a few hours of planned recreation. This will make facing the rest of the day almost tolerable. A rewritten journal from one lazy student's college days should help you in understanding this approach. (Please note that although this "typical" day is directed at male readers, the many insights into time management could be applied easily to the female reader.)

Tuesday

8:00AM Awaken to the joyous sounds of birds gargling and your roommate chirping! Arrgghh! you think - Still in the sleepy middle of a mental muddle - you succumb to sweet slumber.

8:30AM Awake anew. You lie in bed pondering the difficulty of actually waking a gnu. Your mind wanders to memories of last night, the drive-in movie, "Mud Wrestlers from Outer Space versus the Mexican Mole Women" with Kinky Rodriguez and Gunther Montez, the familiar back seat of your faithful '57 chevy and, of course, Betty Lou. Suddenly, you realize that those are someone else's memories...

8:45AM Crawl off to the shower on all threes. Your tennis elbow is still asleep.

9:15AM Return from the shower to primp and preen. It's not a pretty picture!

9:30AM This is your first scheduled time to do nothing. Yeah! You do it very well.

10:15AM Leave for class early so that you can sit in the front row.

10:30AM Sociology 1+1, "Marriage and the Family" - you ask the professor a meaningless question (see page 20). "How can a single old biddy like you, never hitched, never bridled (I bet), teach a course about marriage?" You don't listen to her response but, instead, dream of your happiness --- you cheating on your taxes, your wife cheating on you.

11:20AM Follow the most beautiful girl in class to where she chows down. You chew on the social significance of ambiance at a restaurant like Wendy's as well as your cheeseburger.

11:52AM Wipe your chin. Not from the burger, but the girl.

12:00PM "High Noon" break. If you are going to survive this academic pressure cooker, you must force yourself to relax once in a while. You do nothing for an hour. Very well. Practice makes perfect.

1:00PM — Study time. Blegh!

1:15PM — Enough is enough! You go to class early.

1:30PM — Math Art 101, "Counting by Numbers." It occurs to you that Van Gogh was right, "Sometimes life just doesn't add up."

2:30PM — English 022, "The Beet Poets of San Francisco." You initiate a fake argument (see page 20) with a classmate as to whether these poets were really just Bongophiliacs who couldn't keep a beat or whether they should have been beaten until they were vegetables. You argue, quite persuasively, that they only wrote for the money, the higher celery (#). You Lose.

3:30PM — Study time. You are a glutton for punishment.

4:30PM — Planned recreation. You watch reruns of "Leave it to Beaver," "Hogan's Heroes," and "Get Smart."

6:00PM — Dinner in the dorm. You spend ninety minutes table-hopping from friend to friend so that you can fantasize about every female who reveals a healthy appetite.

7:30PM — Recovery from dinner. You lie down to allow the "don't be gruel" soup and soybean surprise to settle. You chuckle to yourself that if dormitory dinners could be divorced there would never be a just settlement.

8:00PM — Go to bed. Who are you kidding? You don't want to hit the books, you're not a hit with the ladies, and you're afraid you might hit your roommate, so you might as well hit the hay. After all, you're not getting any younger.

Z z z

And so it seems that our pages together have dwindled down to a precious few. If you have learned your lessons well, then you will:

—**Attend class and sit in the front row**
—**Analyze your strengths and weaknesses**
—**Analyze your teacher's strengths and weaknesses**
—**Struggle to become creative in your work**
—**Use the many resources available in the library**
—**Refine your test-taking techniques**
—**Budget your time effectively**

In short, you will become a more successful student. You will still be lazy, but at least you will have the skills to survive the "massacre" of school.

Final Random Thoughts

We must all face the ravages of time, literally and figuratively. Philosophers have written volumes in search of an understanding of this idea of successive existence, infinite duration. However, my grandfather, a Nebraska farmer wisened by the inevitability of the changing seasons, had a penchant for separating the wheat from the chaff.

When asked, "What time is it?" my grandfather would invariably respond with a question, which was, in its own way, the answer that philosophers throughout the ages have failed to discover.

"Time all fools were dead; do you feel ill?"

"Well...do you?

ABOUT THE AUTHOR

Randall James McCutcheon was privileged to attend the college of his banker's choice. Although he subsequently graduated with distinction, his departmental advisor lamented, "If only Randy weren't so lazy, he would have wasted even more time studying."

In the years following graduation, he almost made a living as a graduate teaching assistant, advertising copywriter, radio announcer, and high school teacher.

Mr. McCutcheon was the 1985 Teacher of the Year in Nebraska. In 1985 he received national recognition from the U.S. Dept. of Education and the National Assn. of Secondary School Principals for "innovation in education."

A former student remembers, "Mr. McCutcheon talked real good for a coach. And loud, too."

The book, of course, speaks for itself.

CREDITS

INDEX

May we introduce other Free Spirit books you will find helpful...

FIGHTING INVISIBLE TIGERS
A Student Guide
To Life In "The Jungle"
Earl Hipp

PERFECTIONISM
What's Bad About
Being Too Good
Miriam Adderholdt—Elliott

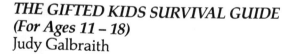

THE GIFTED KIDS SURVIVAL GUIDE
(For Ages 11 – 18)
Judy Galbraith

For ordering information, and to receive a copy of our catalog, write:

Free Spirit Publishing
123 N. Third St., Suite 716
Minneapolis, MN 55401
(612) 338-2068